1 MONTH OF
FREE
READING

at

www.ForgottenBooks.com

By purchasing this book you are eligible for one month membership to ForgottenBooks.com, giving you unlimited access to our entire collection of over 1,000,000 titles via our web site and mobile apps.

To claim your free month visit:

www.forgottenbooks.com/free282927

ISBN 978-0-484-40982-7
PIBN 10282927

THE
Cotton Grader
OR
How to Classify Cotton

A Complete Work

For the Farmer — For Everbody
Teaches Quickly — Teaches Thoroughly

A GUIDE BOOK

THAT

ENABLES THE PRODUCER TO STAND UP IN
THE MARKET—SAY WHAT HE HAS TO SELL
—AND CLAIM HIS RIGHTS.

ARRANGED BY A COMMITTEE OF EXPERT
CLASSIFIERS HAVING THE PRACTICAL EX-
PERIENCE OF MANY YEARS IN ACTIVE
FIELD WORK, AND SENT OUT UNDER THE
AUSPICES OF THE INTERSTATE COTTON
COLLEGE.

EDITED BY N. J. McARTHUR, PRESIDENT OF
THE INTERSTATE COTTON COLLEGE, AND
PUBLISHED BY THE COTTON GRADER
PUBLISHING CO., ATLANTA, GEORGIA.

PRESS OF
CONVERSE & WING PUBLISHING COMPANY
ATLANTA, GEORGIA

INDEX

PREFACE

This Book is intended to give a clear, comprehensive idea of the **Art** of **Cotton Grading** and **Classifying.** As to whether or not that work has been accomplished, he who reads it with the view of learning the **Art** will answer, "Yes." The Fiber is made the unit of classification. Every form and variety of Fiber is described and every character of impurity that might affect it is discussed. As these conditions are shown and explained, the grade or class to which that particular sample or kind of cotton belongs is given. The way of examining is made so plain that any one can understand it.

This is the First **Work** of the kind ever published. Writers, like buyers, have seemingly considered the subject beyond the comprehension of an ordinary **Farmer.** At least for some reason they have acquiesced in the buyers' opinion that grading and naming the price of Cotton was something of which the Farmer should exercise no **primary** judgment. Just a little agitation has aroused the Farmers to a sense of their helplessness in this respect, and when they are told that it requires, in connection with a very short treatise on the subject, only a limited course of practical application in their own homes to make them fairly proficient, they will doubtless profit by the opportunity presented in this small yet complete exposition of the subject. Every Farmer should know how to grade his own cotton. This book will teach him the Art.

THE AUTHORS.

THE COTTON GRADER

COTTON.

As to variety of subjects and quantity of matter, much has been written about Cotton. We have books and volumes of books that tell us about its antiquity, the countries where it may grow, the various kinds of Cotton grown, how and where it is manufactured and how the farmer should plant, fertilize, cultivate, gather, gin and haul it to market. We have books that tell us about machinery for manufacturing the By-Products, others full of statistical and other information, touching upon the future labor to be used in its production, or giving the great Exchange system of fixing its price. In fact, everything from the planting of the seed to the problem of transportation has been written about without limit.

Not Everything.

No; there is one thing about which, as a subject, no line has ever yet before been written. If this effort shall go out to the public, it will be the **First** to appear as a written thesis upon the quesion of **Grading** and **Classifying Cotton.**

The farmer has been instructed in the way best to plant, cultivate and gather, but only by chance has he ever learned the difference between the grades of "Fair" and "Inferior" cotton. He has been educated to hold his cotton for a higher price, but he, the average farmer, does not know whether he is holding "Good Middling" or "Low Ordinary."

It is contended that no valuable instruction of a theoretical character can be given upon the subject of Grading Cotton. This is not true, only as it may mean that a thorough knowledge of the art must combine the practical with the theoretical. It could as reasonably be claimed that a man who is not a college graduate does not know anything, and that no acquaintance with a subject short of a perfect knowledge has any real worth. The idea is absurd. If an expert classifier should say to you that a sample of cotton is of a certain grade and class because its staple is of a given dimension, its color is white, it feels live, flexible and elastic to the touch, its fiber is uniformly good, it shows no injury from previous dampness, it is not stained and it is comparatively clean, could you not see these several and various points of classification as he mentioned them? Suppose next that instead of having the sample in hand, he should simply describe one of that kind, and ask you to select from a lot of cotton before you a bale that would correspond with the described grade, could you not, on first trial, perform the assigned task? Again, if instead of communicating with you, orally, he should write out this description, could you not as well, or better, comply with his request? Could you not soon return to him and say: "Here, Mr. Classifier, is your bale of Middling Cotton"? Assuredly any intelligent man could do this, and what he could do in selecting this grade he could do in selecting any other.

We are creatures of custom. Often men fight,

bleed and die, zealously, heroically and patriotically, defending causes, which, in so far as they may know through personal investigation, might prove unworthy the name. Custom is a tyrant. It is a ruler whose sway is never abated by age. Precedent is a despot, unfeeling, exacting and domineering. "In the way our fathers trod" is a commendable sentiment of veneration, and as a guide for our steps, may have many shining exceptions, but, in the main, the path which should have been lighted by experience remains darkened, and leads us often over a rough and stony road. Who declares that the farmer of the South, he that grows annually twenty bales of cotton, is utterly disqualified, under any character of preparatory effort, to grade his own cotton and know what it may be worth? The answer is, "Custom." How is it, he, the intelligent farmer, man or boy, cannot do this, when almost any city lad with a half season's warehouse experience can do it? The answer is, "Precedent has arranged it so, and precedent must be observed." Why is it these self same cotton growers make no effort to set aside those customs and precedents which are so detrimental to their financial interests? The only answer seems to be that, though it should be quite expensive, they prefer to "Walk in the way our fathers trod." It is presumptiously assumed by the cotton buyer, both agent and principal, that no one else connected with the transaction but the buyer is capable of judging the grade and value of the cotton to be sold and bought. This is tacitly conceded to be a proper assumption by the farmer's commercial neighbors and friends, and by him is helplessly agreed to—all because it has been a custom so to do.

So strongly has habit or precedent established itself in relation to the question of **Cotton Classification,** that the idea of "special professional acquirement or gift" seems to prevail in the face of all logic and argument to the contrary. In a conversation with an old cotton buyer friend the fact was mentioned that this **Guide** to **Cotton Classifying** was being prepared. He expressed surprise that such a work should be undertaken, declaring it wholly impracticable. He went so far as to declare he would not be willing to go upon record and risk his future reputation by making a written description of any grade of cotton. When questioned closely, as to why not, he could not in answer go beyond the illogical word, "unprecedented." However, he admitted that a very great deal of "valuable theoretical" information could be given. "Theoretical" information is exactly the kind proposed to be given, and it is offered with the honest hope that it may prove "valuable." Until the seller and the buyer can meet upon common ground, both knowing the grade and market value of the article to be sold, the man who does not know is wholly at the mercy of the man who does know.

Classification Basis.

Cotton is classified, not according to variety; but by Grades and Types as indicated by the staple and its condition.

Variety means kind, and its designating name refers, principally, to the place, country, or part of the country, where the soil and climate are adapted to the growth of that particular kind of Cotton. Or a variety name may be given to an improved species.

Grade embraces staple, color, condition and quality.

Staple is the measure of the fiber, as to whether it may be long, or short, fine or coarse, strong or weak, with or without natural twist, uniform or irregular, dead or live, elastic or brittle—the whole comprising the qualities of length and strength.

Color in grading applies to white, as a base, and to all the regular shades from that to the brown or Nankin. It does not include stains, fleck-marks, spots or other discolorations.

Condition follows upon a multiplicity of causes.

(1) SOUNDNESS—as indicated by strength of fiber, or by freedom from the effects of present or previous dampness.

(2) FIRMNESS—as it may feel responsively live or dead to the touch—elastic and flexible.

(3) CLEANLINESS—as it may have more or less trash or "dirt."

(4) DISCOLORATION—as from boll-stain—from dampness in seed—from possible soil stain—from the dry burr marks of late picking—from hoop-stain and from oil stain.

(5) MOTES—as from faulty ginning or from immature seed and seed ends.

(6) INEQUALITY—as from mixing different kinds or varieties of seed cotton.

(7) SPOTS—as from mildew or fungoid or from foliage rust-stain; and,

(8) NON-DEVELOPMENT—as shown by the lack of spiral form or natural twist in the fiber and by the unequal length and strength of the fiber resulting from a mixture of ripe, half-ripe and dead staple.

Quality is that estimate of rating which is based upon the combination of staple, color and condition. To tell the quality is to name the grade or classification.

Type.

Type is more properly a manufacturing term as applied to grades, but it is one with which the field classifier must be acquainted. It is a selected grade of cotton about which and with which other approximate grades, higher and lower, may be combined in harmonious blending. This produces a mixture differing from all its component parts, better than the lower but not so good as the higher, and, of course, unlike the original type grade. By this method, classifying by the manufacturer is reduced from the broad range of diversified grades, to a few types which embrace the better part of these grades. The economy attending this order of arrangement gives, from the several grades selected, a uniform finished product; whereas, if each were taken separately, it would, in itself, constitute a specific type. It also enables the manufacturer the more easily to supply himself with stock, as a large bulk of cotton of any given classification is not always readily obtainable.

Types are made up at, or as it may be for, the mills and factories by qualified expert cotton graders. Here you will find an artist who knows his profession. He does not know, necessarily, and he need not care, whether the cotton he must examine so closely is worth in the market one dollar per pound or only one cent per pound, but he does know that the several lots or parcels of cotton he has selected, varying in weight and classification, after being mixed and taken through all the preparatory processes, must produce a combination which shall give, as a finished product, one without noticeable difference from that resulting from a previous combination of a similar character, and, likewise, from others he must make in future to fill a uniform large order.

A knowledge of this kind has been the professioual capital of the field cotton buyer, as a lack of its possession by the cotton producer has long kept him on the roll of the victimized. Ye buyer understands well the art of "putting up" types, and though there could be no harm in "putting up" an honest type, it is barely fair to work the damaging "average up" plan on the farmer, when in most cases it means "average down." Under our present system of handling cotton, the buyer is entitled to his commission or his rightful speculative profits, but the "average up" plan should be stopped by the seller till he, himself, learns how to "average up." Every farmer who grows cotton should know how to grade, classify and type or average up any assorted lot or number of bales he may offer to sell. In the sense here discussed the term type means to average, or to combine different grades for marketing at a "lump figure."

Type is also a term of distinction used by manufacturers to indicate variety. In the American mills, classification we have the Sea Island, some foreign, and the several Uplands varieties each constituting a type.

Varieties of Cotton.

Many exhaustive treatises have been written upon the Botany of Cotton. For a history of the plant these works are referred to, but in this effort no attempt will be made to go beyond the naming of the different foreign and home varieties and showing their textile comparison.

Foreign Cottons.

The Brown Egyptian is a very fine fibered long stapled cotton. It is used in the manufacture of high grade yarns and fabrics, and a considerable quantity is annually imported into the United States for that purpose. All other varieties of Egyptian Cotton are considered inferior.

The China and India cottons are both of very low grade. The China is consumed entirely at home, but India exports a large part of her raw product to Europe.

The South American cottons are of many varieties. The principal two are the Brazilian and the Peruvian. The Brazilian goes chiefly to Europe, but our American manufacturers use a great deal of the Peruvian (red) in the manufacture of special lines and in the making up of types. Other varieties of the South American cotton are classed with the Mexican product and are considered unimportant both in bulk and quality.

American Cotton.

This designation applies only to the product of the United States of North America and the adjacent islands.

· Sea Island is considered an American product. It is grown principally on the islands off the South Atlantic coast. All points of merit considered, it ranks highest in the grades of cotton the world over. Sea Island cotton is grown also on the main land of Florida, Georgia and South Carolina, that of Florida being the best, but still distinguishable as a lower grade than that of the island product.

The American mainland cotton and its many classes or kinds, both native and improved, is next to be mentioned. The quantity of this general variety is greater than that produced by all other parts of the world combined, and the value set upon its middle or basic grade controls the price of cotton in all commercial quarters of the globe.

Sub-Divisions.

The most important of the several divisions or varieties of the American mainland cotton is that known as the Orleans or Gulf. These names embrace a number of included varieties, all, in the market, being understood as virtually the same. Its staple is both long and strong, measuring in length from one inch to one and one-half inches, and having a tensile capacity highly valued by spinners.

Products from the fields of the higher inland river valley lands of Mississippi, Louisiana, Alabama, Arkansas and Tennessee are only slightly inferior to the Orleans, but they constitute a marketable variety.

Texas cotton stands alone as a separate variety. It varies from seven-eights to one inch in length of staple. The product of the Brazos Valley, however, ranks above this rating and is appreciated in both the home and foreign markets much above the commonly accepted Texas variety.

Uplands embraces all that yield coming from the territory not designated as the home of the several special sub-varieties mentioned. Uplands cotton has a staple from three-fourths of an inch to one inch in standard length. . .

A carefully grown, well developed, cleanly gathered, properly ginned and wrapped bale of white Uplands cotton forms the basic center from which all higher or lower grades are determined. Uplands has its many "Improved" varieties, and its sub-varieties are almost as numerous as the varied characters of the soil, the latitude and the altitude of the fields where they are severally grown. Uplands, however varied, is Uplands and a classifier who may be able to grade one of its varieties may as easily grade all of them.

The Principle of Cotton Grading.

In every development there is a basic point from which growth begins. It is well known that a proper solution of any mathematical question depends upon a careful starting with its unit. As applied in mathematics so the rule must be made to operate in all things. If we wish to understand by investigation any given proposition, we must work out from its initial point. We must go to its base for our first and only correct comprehension of its parts. Again there is a law governing the economy of action which prohibits the attempted performance of two different acts at one and the same time. "Do one thing and do it well, then do the second thing and do it better" is a nice old proverb. If you wish to learn the art of grading cotton, and should take up the study, give your attention to that branch of cotton study alone, and let every non-essential collateral element of cotton be put aside for the time. From this preliminary it might be argued that in the cotton seed is the germ, the unit, the initial point from which to move out in the start to study cotton. I have before told you that volumes and volumes have been written upon cotton with our subject, **Cotton Grading**, left out. These writers begin with the seed and have taken you everywhere else but to a knowledge of classifying the staple about which, otherwise, they have written so much.

Our subject, **Cotton Grading**, has its unit, an initial point, a starting place, that is wholly and entirely its own. If from a bale, or any large bulk of cotton, you should take away, part by part, the smallest quantity you could separate from the general mass, in the course of time, though it should be a long time, you would come to a last small part, a single fillament, and this is your Cotton Grading Unit. It is a simple

Fiber.

To learn to classify cotton here your study begins. You must know all about the single fiber and its combinations with other fibers of the same or of different kinds. Despise not the study of small things if you would undertake the consideration of the cotton fiber, for you are to take only one and it is so small that it would require one hundred and forty millions like it to weigh one pound.

The cotton fiber casually observed presents a deceptive appearance. Viewed thus it looks to be a small, long, solid and perfectly round body, but upon closer observation it shows itself as a narrow flattened tube, twisted in form, and in this respect, resembling somewhat a spirally curled hair. The fiber has its tip extremity closed but its base is fastened like a mouth to its mother seed, from which it feeds itself by a capillary process to maturity. Fiber does not taper in form. It has the same diameter in all the parts of its length. It has a large or small cavity, and is flat, or retains more nearly its apparent cylindrical form, according to its full or its imperfect development. A perfect fiber is covered by a thin clinging dust like membrane, called by botanists the "cuticula" or skin. This covering sometimes goes with the fiber through the factory into yarns or other products, but oftener it disappears in the form of gin dust or mill dust. It is comparatively weightless and neither adds to nor detracts from the value of the staple.

Fiber may be fully developed and still be short or long according to its parent variety. The range of length is from one-half inch to two inches. This measure of fiber length is designated its **staple** and is the first item to be considered in grading or assigning value. Other items, however, relating to the fiber construction are to be reckoned. They are the core or diameter and their strength or tensile power of resistance.

The following shows the relative diameter, length, and strength of the fiber belonging to the several varieties presented:

	Length, inches.	Diameter, inches.	Breaking strain, grains.
Sea Island . . .	1.61	.000640	83.9
Orleans	1.02	.000775	147.7
Texas	1.00	.000765	109.5
Uplands	.93	.000763	104.5
Egyptian . . .	1.41	.000665	127.2
Indian	.89	.000894	160.7

This table is given to show that the fiber with the greatest diameter is the strongest and that usually the coarser grades of fiber belong to the shorter staples.

The measure of tension or breaking strain of a single fiber is estimated by spinners to be from five to ten grams or from eighty to one hundred and sixty grains, or an average of about fifty fibers to sustain a pound.

A Closer Study of the Fiber.

Again let the fact be emphasized that the cotton classifier must be perfectly familiar with the unit of classification. Impurities found in cotton are to him a secondary matter. They are usually easily traced and their causes located. Never let any appearance or condition of a cotton sample take you away from a study of the fiber as the part most affected by that condition.

After the cotton boll fully matures and opens, a few days of exposure to air and sunlight are beneficial, in the way of giving to the slower maturing parts of the pod mature development, and to the whole spiral individuality of fiber. But if left longer than this, exposed to heat and air, the fiber will tend to become harsh and brittle, and the longer so left the more perceptible these injuries become. Besides, if strong winds prevail, dust and sand will be blown into the open cotton, and if it should rain much, water stain will follow.

Natural Twist.

The Natural twist of the cotton fiber varies from about two hundred turns to the inch in good grade Uplands to three hundred turns per inch or more in the best Sea Island product. In connection with its length the value of the fiber hinges upon this quality, as in manufacturing the joining process with other fibers depends upon this as an inter-locking principle. Manufacturers use the micro-scope to ascertain exact spiral character, but this does not imply that the ordinary grading classifier, with his natural vision, holding a sample section in hand, could not determine quite well enough for practical purposes the presence or absence of this quality, just in the same way he would form con-clusive opinion as to length, strength and other special characteristics of the fiber under examina-tion.

Unripe Fibers.

In every sample of cotton, from the highest to the lowest grade, half-ripe and totally dead fibers may be found. Nature in many instances may be able to parade its lines of perfection, but as small a quan-tity as a single pound of perfectly developed and matured lint cotton is not to be included on its list. In a single pound of cotton there are about one hundred and forty million separate and dis-tinct developments of independent fiber. In a bale of cotton there are about five hundred pounds. Then, though a bale of cotton may be classed "Fair" or "Extra" or "Good," terms representing the highest classification of the leading three varie-ties, we are not to look for a total absence of any of the defects upon which such classification is based. As to half-ripe and dead fibers, their pres-ence is natural. Blights may fall upon the bearing plant after one-half the bolls have matured in a healthful form. In like manner the bruising or breaking of limbs on a part of the stalk would cause a similar order of variable ripening. Fibers in the same boll do not all mature simultaneously, yet the boll opens to accommodate the ripe and presents the unripe to the picker in its undeveloped state. Therefore, half-ripe and dead fibers are to be looked for naturally in every sample of cotton. Of course, if they should form too great a percentage of the general bulk, which is sometimes the case, a corresponding lower estimate should be made of the grade, but you should know that "Dead Cotton" is a favorite term used by unscrupulous buyers who seek to undergrade. We do not need the microscope to detect the presence of half-ripe or dead fibers in a specimen sample. The half-ripe is shorter than the mature staple and has less spiral turns in proportion to its length. The dead fiber is like a lifeless parasite winding around and clinging to the mature and the half-ripe fibers. A careful examination, suggested by lacking elasticity and flexibility, will show the grader these qualities. If only the normal quantity is found they may be passed unnoticed, but if they appear in exaggerated form the grade is to be correspondingly lowered.

Broken Fiber.

The inferior or unfit condition of a gin, or the rapidity of its revolution causes the saw-gin to double cut the fiber, taking it from the seed in two sections or leaving a part of the fiber with the seed. This does not occur with the use of the roller gin, used for long staple cotton, but sometimes, with it, there is a rude rupture of the fiber noticeable. With a saw-gin this defect would almost certainly go through the entire bale under examination, and perhaps through many others. It is easily discovered and detracts considerably from an otherwise good grade of cotton.

Stained Fiber.

One drop of ink in a glass of clear water utterly mars the purity of its appearance. A less proportionate part of stained cotton in any sized sample would indicate a greater apparent departure from perfection. One stained fiber in a small pinch of cotton, pulled through the fingers of the examiner shows like a multitude of wriggling rainbows circling a section of clearly outlined horizon. Stains, whether important or unimportant, are good capital for the decrying buyer, who would take advantage, in a purchase from the uninformed producer. Under the head of "Conditions," on a preceding page, are enumerated and named the different kinds of lint stain, considered by the field buyer, in his deals with the farmer and the country merchant. Here I shall refer to the commercial stain only.

Boll Stain.

Boll stain is caused by water that has entered a partly opened boll and saturated the inner pod. The coloring matter from the inner membrane is washed into the general lower body of the pod and gives to it a red or brown shade. This is considered of not much importance, as in the manufacturing processes of dying and sizing such stains would disappear.

Hoop Stains.

Hoop Stain is nothing more nor less than iron band rust and really, in itself, amounts to only the loss of a few ounces of cotton to the bale. However, it suggests a character of neglect or want of care pointing to other impurities, and forms of damage, and furnishes a good excuse or cause for lowering a grade.

Oil Stain.

Oil Stain is caused by the crushing of seed in the gin; the exuding oil giving to the fiber a yellowish color. If this staining should be general throughout the parts of a bale of cotton its value would be much reduced. Its waxy and glue-like nature retards the process of carding and spinning, and such cotton is often wholly rejected by spinners. A second kind of oil stain is only a **probable stain** manifesting its almost certain future appearance in the form of immature seed in the meshes of baled cotton. Separation at the mills is a task too difficult to be undertaken, and if left in, they are crushed by the mill machinery and regular oil stain is the result. "Seeded lint," as it is called, and oil stained cotton are to be graded alike.

Fungoid Stain.

Fungoid stain is but another name for mildewed cotton. It may follow as a result from a number of causes. It ranks with "Damaged Cotton," and there is no special grade to which it may be assigned.

Fiber in Bulk.

Fiber in bulk is cotton lint in large or small quantity, or a mass of fibers taken in aggregate form. In treating fiber in bulk, the single fiber is supposed to have passed examination as the basis of staple, or as it is to be considered the representative of the general class of fibers forming the larger mass to be graded as a whole. Cleanliness and soundness are now the points to be considered.

Broken Leaves.

The leaves of the cotton plant, and sometimes bearded or hard stemmed grasses in badly cultivated fields, are natural factors in reducing the value and grade of cotton. A dry leaf in close proximity to the open boll is very frequently included in the hand grasp of the hurrying picker. If it is not removed, it goes with the mass of seed cotton through the gin and is broken or cut into small fragments. The smaller these particles of leaf are made by the gin, the more thoroughly they become mixed with the fiber, and the more difficult they are to remove in the preparatory processes at the mills. The larger pieces may fall out of their own weight, and on this account are not considered so injurious to the grade, but the smaller ones remain, and, if very fine, are considered a clinging and inseparable impurity. The skeleton of the leaf, too, a stick-like tissue, often becomes a part of the foreign mass. It is classed "inseparable," and is, therefore, correspondingly objectionable. These impurities, as you see, are themselves to be graded. If the cotton sample shows leaf trash in large pieces without the stem or skeleton accompaniment, its grade is not badly affected, but, if the trash shows in the form of smaller pepper-like particles, or has the stick cuttings, a careful grader will mark it down.

Broken Seeds.

This constitutes what is known as one of the "Heavy Impurities" of cotton. Broken seeds are usually covered with lint or fiber ends, and these becoming interlocked with other fibers are difficult to remove. In Grading, these impurities are called "Shell" or "Bearded Motes." The surplus parts of body or fatty ends of seed are often cut into the lint roll by close ginning. These pieces are also called "shell," and rank with heavy impurities. Cotton affected by these impurities is to be graded with the lower type of "Broken Leaf" cotton.

.(Note if the fungus end above mentioned should carry a part of the main body of the seed. In such case, oil stain would result.)

Sand and Soil.

The winds sometimes fill, or, as it is termed, "load" open cotton in the bur with sand, and again, often it is blown or knocked out upon the ground and becomes impregnated, more or less, with sand and other earth matter. This affects only the weight of the cotton and not its quality, unless soil stain or mildew should follow. Spinners, however, claim that the extra frictional wear to machinery and the danger incurred from fire render it less desirable and, therefore, it is brought to a lower grade.

Dampness.

Dampness or moisture is not to be considered an impurity, only as it may become the possible producing agent of mildew or rot. To form these there must be a meeting of the damp parts of a bale of cotton with the air from without. Such meeting would afford the needed means for evaporation, and thereby the cause of decay or rot would, in the main, be removed. Cotton dry enough to gin, if immediately compressed would be safe from serious harm to be occasioned by dampness. Even cotton "wet down" in the compressing or baling process would suffer little injury therefrom, as evaporation would be very rapid. If, however, the place of storage should be damp, or if by constant exposure to water and exterior dampness, evaporation should be prevented, **mildew** would follow and **rot** would be the result. Cotton is a great absorbent. A bale of cotton placed over an evaporating pool will drink in dampness like a thirsty animal drinking water. Continued absorption with the avenues of evaporation closed would soon reduce the fiber and deaden its twist. With its quality of elasticity thus destroyed it is in the first stage of decomposition.

In grading a bale of damp cotton, if the moisture is found to be only near the surface, procure a specimen sample below the damp part and classify as if no water had been observed. In weighing, the proper deduction for water-weight can be made. If the dampness should extend into the interior of the bale, the classifier is placed in a dilema. Exeessive dampness disturbs normal elasticity and he will be able to judge of this quality only as a collateral adjunct of the length and strength of the staple under examination. He will be able easily to know whether this dampness is new or fresh or whether it is an old water sob. If the latter, the form and strength of the staple, besides the changes before mentioned, will show rank abnormal differences in fibers of apparently even development. Parts of the same sample in dried form will show different degrees of elasticity, and an unmistakable odor of mustiness will manifest itself. Cotton in this condition, no matter what it once may have been, is now to be graded "Inferior." If, on the contrary, the bale should appear to be generally damp, and otherwise sound, its grade is not affected and a deduction for water-weight from the bulk weight of the bale is all that need be done in fairness to seller and buyer.

Structural Composition.

In a work on Grading and Classifying it is not necessary to go into the "Chemistry" of the cotton staple. However, as the laws of Fermentation, Decomposition, Fungi, etc., operate with more or less force according to the physical stability of the substance to be acted on, any one desiring thus further to investigate is referred to chemistry as applied to these questions, and in that connection, the following structural analysis of cotton is given:

Fiber,	83.71 per cent.
Water,	6.74 per cent.
Free Nitrogen,	5.79 per cent.
Ash,	1.65 per cent.
Protein,	1.50 per cent.
Fat,	.61 per cent.

100.

Porosity is a general property of matter, but the surface pores of a single fiber of cotton are too nearly allied in magnitude to the atomic nature of their surroundings to give passage way to the combined elements composing water. Hence moisture of cotton is due wholly to fiber-layer and capillary avenues of ingress.

Dryness.

In connection with Dampness is to be considered a principle of Dryness, that affects the worth of cotton. A sample of cotton of average high grade, in its normal state, contains nearly seven per cent. water. Immerse it in a vessel of water till it becomes thoroughly saturated, then expose it to the air and sun for a few hours and it would show only its normal quantity or part of water. Subject it next to a heating process. Confine it in a bake-oven or other drying place till, as nearly as possible all moisture is driven out, expose it again to the air and from that element it would soon absorb moisture enough to have its original normal quantity. It is this quality of dampness that enables the classifier to judge, through its character of elasticity and flexibility, the presence or absence of the necessary vitality in a sample under examination. A healthful well developed capillary state of the staple gives a normal condition of dampness. This in turn through the elasticity and flexibility of a sample containing it proves and shows the origin of its presence.

Flexibility.

As a rule flexibility indicates strength of fiber, though short, coarse and strong staples are rather more harsh than flexible. A sample of the latter kind, in response to the touch or clasp of the hand, will show sufficient capillary (cavity) force to indicate its right position in the line of grades. If from any cause a sample staple should show a quality of dryness below that of the normally damp stage, it would be indicated by a harsh brittle yielding to the touch, and upon closer examination it would be found wanting in some of the characteristic essential points of good grade.

Grades of Cotton.

In an American cotton crop of twelve million bales, if graded by the bale, it may be truthfully asserted that twelve million different and varying grades would be found. In other words, no two bales could be found that would sample "through and through" or "out and out" in exact likeness. Notwithstanding this fact, there might be found, say, one-third of this number of bales that would be so nearly alike as to be classed together as one type or grade. Another smaller fractional lot, better or worse, higher or lower, finer or coarser, might be found that could be placed into another grade. And so on, other fractional parts of the twelve million bales might be found having a general bulk likeness and similar grade quality, till the whole could be embraced in about twenty of these fractional divisional like parts. These twenty or more parts might again be sub-grouped into seven or eight distinct quality divisions, designated "Full Grades," with which higher or lower approximately similar grades may be typed, to compose a bulk lot of cotton of a required given classification. These approximates are designated "Half" and "Quarter" grades.

The American Exchange Market.

As an American proposition, both the classification of cotton and the price to be paid for it are regulated by a class who have no interest, whatever, either in its production or its manufacture. We have two great commercial or market "Exchanges" located respectively in New York and in New Orleans. Seats in these "Exchanges" are of high commercial value, and are of a limited number. The membership composing them is supposed to be "strictly" American, but it may be remarked, soto-voce, that the supposition is "strictly" a supposition. From these places the men who have no part in producing, hauling or manufacturing cotton, designate the terms by which its differing grades shall be known, and dictatorially declare what the market price shall be. This is only another way of showing our American disposition to bow to "custom," respect established "precedents," and "walk in the way our fathers trod." But the right or wrong of this custom is not a matter to be discussed here.

Grade Classification.

According to American Classification .there are seven full grades of the mainland varieties with which, however, neither the Florida nor the Georgia and South Carolina long or Sea Island staples are to be included. These seven grades are: Fair, Middling Fair, Good Middling, Middling, Low Middling, Good Ordinary and Ordinary. Fair is the highest and best grade and, therefore, there can be no half or quarter grades above it, but, descending, all other grades have half or quarter grades both above and below them. The complete table of American grades used until recently by the commercial world is as follows:

(1) FAIR, Barely Fair, Strict Middling Fair and Fully Fair.

28

(2) MIDDLING FAIR, Barely Middling Fair, Strict Good Middling and Fully Good Middling.

(3) GOOD MIDDLING, Barely Good Middling, Strict Middling and Fully Middling.

(4) MIDDLING, Barely Middling, Strict Low Middling and Fully Low Middling.

(5) LOW MIDDLING, Barely Low Middling, Strict Good Ordinary and Fully Good Ordinary.

(6) GOOD ORDINARY, Barely Good Ordinary and Strict Ordinary.

(7) ORDINARY, Low Ordinary and Inferior.

This system, or catalog, of classifying terms is as old almost as the American cotton market itself. When the American cotton exchanges first were established, about thirty-five years ago, they adopted and used the old classifying terms. But within recent years they have dropped out the five grades below Good Ordinary, and have substituted or added thirteen new terms. These added terms are: (1) Strict Good Middling Tinged. (2) Good Middling Tinged. (3) Strict Middling Tinged. (4) Middling Tinged. (5) Strict Low Middling Tinged. (6) Low Middling Tinged. (7) Strict Good Ordinary Tinged. (8) Fully Middling Stained. (9) Middling Stained. (10) Barely Middling Stained. (11) Strict Low Middling Stained. (12) Fully Low Middling Stained, and (13) Low Middling Stained. Middling is still made the basis of value, and Good Middling Tinged is placed on a par with it. The regular classification in its revised form, showing the 1907-1908 variation of values is given on next page. The difference in value therein quoted is rather more basic than arbitrary, and is changed as the demand may increase or decrease for a specific type of cotton.

New York Differences in Grade.

	CENTS.	
Fair	1.75	on
Strict Middling Fair	1.50	"
Middling Fair	1.25	"
Barely Middling Fair	1.00	"
Strict Good Middling	.75	
Fully Good Middling	.62	..
Good Middling	.50	..
Barely Good Middling	.37.	
Strict Middling	.25	
Middling	Basis	
Strict Low Middling	.30	off
Fully Low Middling	.65	"
Low Middling	1.00	"
Barely Low Middling	1.25	"
Strict Good Ordinary	1.50	"
Fully Good Ordinary	1.75	"
Good Ordinary	2.00	"
Strict Good Middling Tinged	.35	on
Good Middling Tinged	Value of Mid.	
Strict Middling Tinged	.20	off
Middling Tinged	.30	"
Strict Low Middling Tinged	1.00	"
Low Middling Tinged	1.50	"
Strict Good Ordinary Tinged	2.00	"
Fully Middling Stained	1.00	"
Middling Stained	1.25	"
Barely Middling Stained	1.75	"
Strict Low Middling Stained	2.25	"
Fully Low Middling Stained	2.62	"
Low Middling Stained	3.00	"

Tinge.

The term "Tinge" or "Tinged" as applied in this classification refers to natural color only, and not to any stain or dye from extraneous causes. The color of cotton is strongly marked by the character of the soil upon which it is produced. Dingy gray, cream, yellowish brown and other shades are common departures from white, which 'is the color quality of the best grades.

Sea Island Cotton.

Sea Island cotton is classed in only two (American) varieties and seven grades. The varieties are the Island proper and the Mainland. A distinction between the Florida product and that of Georgia and Carolina is sometimes made. This would give a third variety. The grades are: **Extra Fine, Fine, Medium Fine, Good Medium, Medium, Common** and **Ordinary.**

Egyptian and India cotton, and the South American product have each a large number of varieties, but a limited order of grade classifications. In this work it 'is not at all necessary to quote these points specifically, as its' scope is intended to embrace only the American classification.

Grading and Light.

Again we are brought to the unit of classification, the fiber. To judge properly the character of a sample staple, we must be able to see it under favorable conditions. Since it is a reflection of the direct ray of light falling upon an object that brings it to view, the best view is to be obtained by making the line of vision and the line of direct ray to coincide. That is, in homely parlance, we must look at an object from the direction the light comes. In this, the latitude of the American cotton-belt, the sun in his path of apparent travel from east to west, sheds an inclining or direct ray from the south. In the open, that is, at the wagon on the street, the bulk of the cotton crop is first sampled. Here the experienced buyer, if the day is cloudless, will turn his back to the sun, and proceed with his inspection. But if the day should be partly cloudy, so that direct rays from the sun would be obstructed, he would turn from the sun to the largest belt of open skylight presented, to obtain its reflected rays as a best light for examination. On the outside, however, the eye of the experiencd or inexperienced examiner would doubtless accommodate itself to the best light conditions, the only difference being that the examiner with experience would take his position naturally and quickly, whereas the other might move in the line of experiment. Off the street—within walls or under shelter—with samples on the board, the item of good light is all important. Light openings, admitting direct rays from the south, southeast or southwest, are usually too beaming. Similar objection may be raised to the overhead light, on account of its "borrowed" glare. The best light, then, is that to be reflected on a bright day from an open clear expanse of northern skylight. This affords a soft mellow light, such as best enables the examiner to discern the shades of color.

Color.

The highest grade of cotton is naturally bleached and must be perfectly white. Cotton having a corresponding quality of staple, cleanliness, flexibility, and general purity, but showing a gray, cream, or brownish cast would be considered "off color," or, as it is termed in the newer classification, "Tinged." Cotton that is tinged cannot be classed with any one of the highest four grades—that is, with Fair, Strict Middling Fair, Middling Fair and Barely Middling Fair. The name, "Fair," being given to these grades, as we may understand, precludes the possibility of "Tinge." Cottons of equivalent grade in every particular, except color, vary about one-half cent per pound in favor of the white grade. In the "Grade List" issued by the New York Cotton Exchange September, 1907, Good Middling was rated one-half cent higher than Middling. On the same list Good Middling Tinged is given the same value as Middling Untinged. This order of difference in value prevails throughout the list and is to be accepted as a law which fixes the color variation of value at one-half cent per pound.

Vision and Touch.

Vision and touch are the co-operative agents in the work of classification. The eye and the hand move in harmony to a quick and practical decision. A representative sample is procured by the examiner. He plucks from the larger parcel a smaller quantity in a seemingly careless manner, yet he gives the very closest observation to the particles of fiber as they may kink, twist about, cling together, and show such other characteristic resistance or yielding to separation as would indicate certain points of grade. He compresses the detached smaller part in his single hand, noting, the easy pliability, velvety softness, naturally live moist touch, or, as it may be their opposites, harshness, dryness and brittleness, judging in a moment the presence or absence of that flexibility, elasticity and responsiveness which give vigor and strength to the staple body. He turns again to the staple. With thumb and finger he separates or pulls apart a smaller portion that he may see the length of the fiber, and judge by its resistance to separation its general quality of strength. He will note that the fiber is of uniform length or not; that is, coarse or fine, that the layers lie in parallel line or departing angle, the presence or absence of gin cut and dead fibers, and particularly will he note the spirality or movement and the quick or slow action of the ends of the separated fibers, as they coil and move back to the bulk which has retained them. Again he will turn to the general sample. Of its dampness and soundness he has already judged. He looks for impurities. He sees broken leaves, sticks, shells and stains, or he does not see them. He may find much foreign substance and impurity, and he may find only the few that are termed natural. In the meantime color has been determined, and the whole question of classifying that grade has been settled.

In the matter of **Grading** cotton the governing principle is the character of the staple. With good vision and touch it is easy to know its quality. Then, as a rule, first locate the exact Grade of the staple, and place it in that classification regardless of whatever defects it may carry. Next, proceed to list its impurities. If it has no impurities or defects, it belongs in the grade assigned to its staple, but if it has note them, one by one, and reduce the classification accordingly.

Where the Farmer Stands.

You will observe that under the present classification the white grades range from "Fair," the highest, to "Good Ordinary," the lowest, embracing in number seventeen grades. The quoted difference in value of the extreme grades is three and three-fourths cents, or an average of nearly one-quarter of a cent per grade. Grading cotton, in so far as the farmer is concerned, is either a ridiculous farce, or cotton buyers, as a class, are superior morally to ordinary humanity. There are doubtless many honest grading buyers, but many does not mean all by a great number. The opportuniy is afforded, and the temptation is great. The farmer does not know, and if he is willing to prove his satisfaction with a "top of the market" sale by "setting up" dinner to the buyer after the transaction, all conscience twinges are alleviated. Let us take a good "Uplands" producing county in any one of the states and from September and October clean pickings of well matured good stapled white cotton suppose 2,000 bales shall be marketed. According to these conditions 1,500 of these bales ought to be graded "Strict Good Middling," some of them higher. The chance would be, however, that not one in the entire lot would be graded above "Middling" and many of them below that grade. Middling is the basis of the market quotation, and the farmer who gets the highest quoted price and returns to his neighbors with the boast, "I got the top of the market for the most of mine," is the victim. In such a case the actual loss to this one county of cotton growers would exceed $5,000. Yet, year after year it is done, and thus it has become a custom. While digressing in this line it is proper to state that the spinner—the manufacturer—is not a party to this one-sided deal. When the cotton is presented to him, every grade and type is priced according to its value—no more and no less. In this latter transaction all parties are equally well informed. But the poor farmer! Where was he? In all his long life he has not had even one little short week to give to   •

A Study of Classification.

Keeping in mind the fact that perfect staple and absolute freedom from impurities are not to be expected in the highest typed bale of cotton, we have none the less a standard highest grade. From this grade to the basis, the middle or medium grade between the highest and the lowest, including "Strict Good Middling Tinged," there are ten steps of descent. If we should take a bale of our best stapled and cleanest white cotton and grade · it "Fair," there must be some falling off either in quality of staple or character of purity, or both, to make the first descending step to "Strict Middling Fair." There might not appear any additional impurity and the staple might be as good, yet different, and the grade is not the same. The long fibered more fragile but finer fillament would take precedence over the shorter, coarser and stronger staple with which it would be compared. As we would come down the line, at each step we should find changes in the classification occurring from difference in length and strength, lack of uniformity and other previously mentioned inequalities of the staple.

The Basis.

"Middling," the medium or middle quality between "Fair" and "Ordinary," is the basis of classification. Given a sample of white, firm, elastic and flexible bulk fiber having staple of uniform measure from three-fourth of an inch to one inch in length, with a minimum showing of broken leaf, and without stain or any of the heavy impurities of shell, motes, etc., and we should have an accepted grade of "Middling." Observe there is a difference between "broken" leaf and "peppered" leaf. The latter in its pulverized form is considered a very objectionable impurity, as previously explained. No sample carrying powdered leaf in quantity, or stem trash could be classed "Middling."

All classifications, higher than Middling, are supposed to be unaffected by the slight impurities they may carry. But from "Middling" through the descending grades impurities are an important consideration. Staple still holds its priority. But even a good staple loses its finer character when associated with impurities. The quality of the staple falls off, or the impurities increase, or both, in the old classification, from "Middling" to "Inferior." "Inferior" grades are usually from late piekings of short-developed or half-open frost bitten bolls. The staple is of the lowest type, and the fiber is nearly always stained. "Inferior" has its descending grades through a varying line from bad to worse, known as "Dog-tails."

All strict commercial classification lies between the grades of from "Fair" to "Good Ordinary." These represent the extreme variations in value of about four cents. Below the grade of Ordinary,

"Tinge," or the natural color of the cotton does not affect its grade. From this point it is purely a question of staple and impurity. In this matter, if the staple is comparatively good or bad the accompanying impurities would govern its valuation. The whole list of impurities has been given on a preceding page, as well as their respective degrees of damaging character. A careful study of the question of Impurities should be made. "The last of the crop" is supposed to be **gradeless,** but not so; it is only gradeless as it affords the buyer an opportunity to place his knowledge against the inexperience of the seller. Where one knows and the other guesses, the guesser is the loser. The shrewd buyer not only grades this kind of cotton, but he also grades the man who offers it for sale. That is, he sizes up the one and undergrades the other, much to his own satisfaction and profit.

Codes.

We have only a few very large cotton firms who buy directly from the producer, yet the whole field is covered by them. Instead of the usual terms of commercial classification, each of these firms has a "Code" made up of letters or figures to represent the different classifications. These "Codes" are used only in one way, and that is in the deal between these same buyers, or their agents, and the farmers or producers. When the turn is made by them to the regular market these "Code" classifications are dropped, and the regular market terms are employed. Imagine the blank look that would shade the face of any regular market buyer if you should offer him a lot of cotton and tell him that it ought to class all around, fours or fives or Bs or Ds. He would no more understand you than if you were to address him in Chinese. These "Codes" are admitted to be variable; that is, subject to change, as to the precise grades represented at all times. In several of the states, the State of Georgia for instance, the arbitrary "Code" of one firm of cotton buyers is the only classification known.

Granting the probability that no imposition has been practiced through this method of grading, still a uniform basis of classification, understood by all, would be better. Then again, if, say, "fours" in Alabama is not "fours" in South Carolina, what would be "fours" in Georgia? If I should fix a "Code" grading "Fours" as Middling and you should so understand it and, later for my convenience, I should change "Fours" to "Good Middling," to say the least, you would not have a clear conception of the market grades. It is generally conceded that a uniform universally accepted system of grading by number would be better than the present, but until such time as this may be done, let us cling to the old system. In the present system of private Codes in use the numbers range from ones for "Fair" to fours for "Middling," and eights and ten for the ordinary and inferior grades. The numbers employed, however, run much higher, as the lower grades are to be designated.

A Quotation.

Charles William Burkett, Professor of Agriculture in the State College of North Carolina, in his work entitled, **"Cotton,"** published in 1906, comments on the respective situations of producer and buyer as follows:

"Ordinarily the judgment rests solely with the

buyer. He classes fiber as he thinks it should be classed, or as he chooses to class it, and offers a market price for that grade of cotton. You can readily see that where only a single buyer is present, and especially if that one be unscrupulous to some degree, a considerable loss may come to the producer and a corresponding gain to the buyer. Naturally there are tricks in buying cotton as there are tricks in other trades, and honesty and business integrity find recognition in the cotton market as they do elsewhere in life:

"The most satisfactory selling is done where several buyers are on hand, and this competition, as a rule, means the highest price will be offered. Of course even in this case buyers may join hands and one do the most of the buying one day, another a second day, and so on, each taking his turn and getting his cotton at the lowest price. . But the daily paper now gives the farmer the prices in the leading markets of the world, and with the railways making transportation to better markets easy, he usually secures what the product is worth, or at least the market value of the grade in which it is classed."

The "But" above, referring to daily papers and railways, loses all its force in the concluding words of the paragraph, which are, "Or at least the market value of the grade in which it is classed." Yes, classed by the buyer and not the seller.

Advisory.

Let any farmer or any other person who wishes to take up this study read this little book over carefully, if possible, keeping a full variety of samples before him. Every single reading of the descriptions, and comparisons made as directed would be equivalent almost to a season's active work in a warehouse, falling only a little short of a practical experience. A full variety of samples may be procured by addressing the publishers of this work.

WARNING

Every page, every line, every word and every syllable comprising the contents of this little book, "The Cotton Grader, or How to Classify Cotton," is protected by copyright. To a majority of those into whose hands it may fall this announcement will have no significance. But there are others. It is contemplated that the information it may convey shall go out directly from its authors to the individuals to be benefitted thereby. This does not mean that any person desiring to possess a copy would be barred from obtaining it from the publishers or through the legitimate channels of trade. It means that any appropriation of the work, in parts or as a whole, to be used, **secondarily,** for the promotion of private educational enterprises would be an infringement. Let those concerned be governed accordingly.

THE PUBLISHERS.

THE
INTER-STATE COTTON COLLEGE

The Inter-state Cotton College will give a thorough course in the Art of **Grading Cotton**. It is the first school of the kind to be established, and is the only Cotton Classifying school now on the Globe. Its promoters were first to see the necessity for such an Institution, and they were first to move in the direction of waiting upon that demand. They will furnish every facility for a thorough practical education in the lines of instruction to be given.

The announcement and extensive advertisement of this college work has suggested to others the establishing of so-called "correspondence schools." By this method, if honestly conducted, a measure of knowledge pertaining to the subject may be imparted. However, it is not only more expensive, but it is less beneficial than a course taken under the personal and present supervision of a competent instructor.

In a **Home Course** samples of every possible grade and type of cotton should be furnished, with a clearly written minute explanation of the characteristic points of each, with its variations from, and mergeable relations with, approximate grades. This is exactly what the unstable "tell you how" cor-

43

respondence schools will not undertake to do. The Inter-state College has the best advantages in the matter of securing and making up **Samples of Grades,** and will furnish a complete "Budget" of these samples to any one who cannot, at present, conveniently attend the' College and take a more practical course. The **Terms** of the home or "Budget" course permits the student to attend the College at any future time, however remote, and receive **free** such later and better training as he might need or desire. That is, the terms of a correspondence course would inelude an unlimited scholarship course in the College.

If you wish to take up the study of Cotton Grading and Classifying, do not adopt any **Half-way** means. **G**et the best. For either the College Practical Training or the Sample Budget and Home Instruction Course apply to the Inter-state Cotton College, Atlanta, **G**eorgia.

CPSIA information can be obtained
at www.ICGtesting.com
Printed in the USA
BVHW04*1050170918
527708BV00015B/2081/P